Market Data Downloading

A quick-start guide to sourcing and downloading financial
data from Bloomberg, Reuters, Markit and the Internet
using Excel, VBA and R

Thomas P Reid

I0477981

AUTHOR'S NOTE:

As you read this ebook you will see that there are a number of web-sites mentioned. All were **"alive"** at the time of writing but it cannot be guaranteed that they always will be. Although I have never had a problem using any of them, feel free to run a virus and/or malware checker against them before use if you have any concerns. A nice utility for this can be found at https://safeweb.norton.com/. I know what you're thinking, how do I know that website's safe? Well, you've got to have faith in something otherwise it's turtles all the way down!

If you spot any mistakes, omissions or have any comments or questions regarding the content of this eBook please contact me via email on taupirho@gmail.com

Dedicated to my family

CONTENTS

Copyright:

Disclaimer:

Trademarks:

Author's Note:

1 Introduction

    About the Author

    Who is this guide for?

    What this guide is.

    What this guide is not.

2 Downloading from Bloomberg

    Downloading data using the Bloomberg Excel Addin

    The Bloomberg Data Point (BDP) Function

    The Bloomberg Data Set (BDS) Function

    The Bloomberg Data History (BDH) Function

    Using the API functions from VBA

    Downloading data using the COM data control

    Downloading data using the new and improved data control

    Controlling Bloomberg using DDE

    The Bloomberg Data Licence Builder

3 Downloading from Thomson Reuters

    Downloading data using Excel and the RDATA command

    Downloading data using The ADFIN analytic functions

Other Reuters Data Sources

Datascope Select

Datascope Bulk Equity

Reuters WorldScope

4 Downloading from Markit

Using cURL.

Via FTP.

Using Visual Basic

5 Some more useful sources of Data

Google Finance

Downloading from Google Finance via Excel Web Query

Yahoo Finance

Downloading data from Yahoo finance

Automating the loading of finance data from Yahoo into Excel

Quandl

Downloading data from Quandl using its API

Downloading data from Quandl using R

A web-site for intraday historical FOREX tick data

Getting data using general web scraping techniques

About the Author

Hello and welcome to this guide. I have been a software developer for over 25 years, the most recent of which have been in the employ of some of the world's largest financial institutions. As such I have built up considerable experience of the finance world and more importantly in the processing and manipulation of financial data. I decided to write this guide for two main reasons. First of all I wanted to fill a knowledge gap. There really isn't that much good material out there describing what this guide does, even in this wondrous time of knowledge being on tap 24x7 online. Secondly I wanted a permanent record of this knowledge just for myself, something I could refer to and know it would always be there should I need it rather than writing things down on scraps of paper and losing them just when I needed them most. I would have loved to have had access to an eBook like this years ago.

Who is this guide for?

This guide should appeal to anyone who works in the financial sector and who regularly has to deal with, store or in some way process the myriad types of financial data available from various market data providers and the wider internet. My main focus is on three of the biggest and most popular data vendors, namely Bloomberg, Reuters and Markit. The reason for this is that these are the data providers that I know, have experience of and use on a daily basis. Hopefully once you see how relatively easy it is to get data from these providers it will spur you on to experiment with other data vendors not mentioned here that you or your organisation use most.

In addition to the more established names mentioned above which are generally a realistic option only for those actually working in the finance industry, there are now a number of useful websites which allow those who do not have access to specialised terminals and software to download various financial data sets. Google, Yahoo and Quandl are among the best well known of these so I show how to get data from them too.

What this guide is.

In a nutshell, this guide will, through numerous worked examples mainly using EXCEL and VBA, show you how to source and automate the downloading of financial data from some of the most popular financial data vendors and the world-wide web too. Most of the example code in this guide uses a combination of Excel and VBA but I also touch on the use of FTP, cURL - which is a kind of FTP/HTTP hybrid utility - and the R programming language.

What this guide is not.

This is a quick-start guide *not* an in-depth reference text. Its main aim is to show you the basics with enough explanation and examples to give you a good grounding in the techniques required. Much of the more advanced topics associated with the subject are either not covered or even mentioned. For many of you what *is* covered will be more than enough for you to get started and do useful things. For others I hope it will give you a solid foundation and the confidence to take it the next level should you need to.

This guide will also **not** discuss how to use EXCEL or program in VBA or R, nor will it show you how to install any required software. In fact I make many assumptions about you and the environment you will be programming in. The most important of these being:-

- My most important assumption of all is that you have all the necessary logins, permissions, licensing agreements etc. required for you to legally access and/or download data in the first place, regardless of the source of that data.

- You have access to a PC that has legal and valid Bloomberg and/or Reuters installation on it along with all their various components needed to use their application programming interfaces (API's) and a reasonably up-to-date version of Excel. All the examples in this document use Excel 2003. The version of R used is 3.3.1.

- Your PC should also have access to the web although this isn't strictly required if you're not going to be downloading data from Markit, Yahoo, Google or Quandl

- You have at least a passing knowledge of the data you are retrieving and the systems you are retrieving it from. So that for instance I would expect you to know what is meant by a stock's bid price or a bond's coupon rate for example.

- You are comfortable surfing the web, using EXCEL and have at least some experience of programming in VBA, although none of the examples are particularly difficult to follow.

Before starting, you should also note that the data vendors – particularly Bloomberg in my experience - can and **will** monitor your data download volumes and may take steps to restrict downloads altogether if they feel you are misusing their systems, and/or other punitive action. In extremis I guess they could simply switch off their data feed altogether. They usually also have quite strict licensing conditions attached to the data you do download. For example it's normally a requirement that any data that is downloaded has to remain on the PC it was downloaded from. If in any doubt, check with your organisation's legal and/or risk and compliance control function before doing anything.

Bloomberg is the most popular financial data provider in the world. Its eponymous terminals are used in almost all financial institutions of any note. If you work for a bank, insurance company, pension provider or fund manager it's likely there will be a number of Bloomberg terminals in and around your place of work.

Downloading data using the Bloomberg Excel Addin

One of the most popular tools for enabling the retrieval of Bloomberg financial data into Excel is the Bloomberg Excel Add-in. To recap, add-ins are software libraries that you can add in (hence the name) to Excel to enable it to do things it would otherwise not be able to. So before going any further make sure that you have the Bloomberg Excel add-in installed. Once it's installed, a new item labelled Bloomberg will become available in the list of main Excel menu items. It should look something like figure 2.1 shown below although yours may be a bit different depending on which version of Excel and/or the API you're running.

figure 2.1

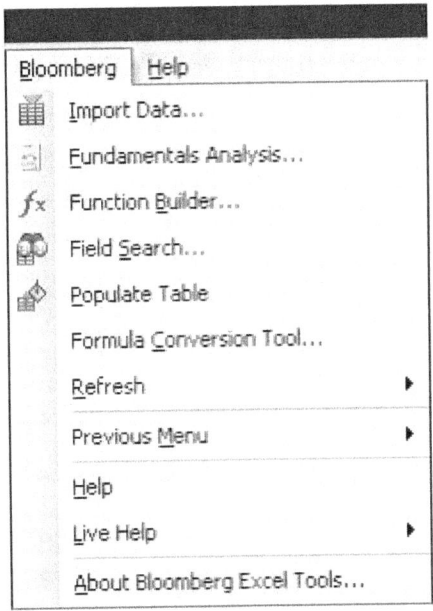

Additionally you should also see that a new toolbar has become available. The icons displayed in the toolbar and the new menu Items shown in figure 2.1 allow you to build up data queries step-by-step against the Bloomberg database for display in your Excel spreadsheet. I won't explore the functionality of these items further but they can be useful for beginners to build up their knowledge and confidence in using the various Bloomberg tools within Excel. What we will explore is what is behind these extra commands, namely the Bloomberg API functions. These functions expose three important new formulas that can be typed straight into the cells of Excel to display Bloomberg data and since this is so, it also means they can be manipulated programmatically via Excel's built-in language VBA. But before examining them from a programming perspective let's look at each API call in a bit more detail and how you would use them by typing them into Excel just like you would any other regular Excel function such as SUM or AVG for example.

The Bloomberg Data Point (BDP) Function

The syntax of this is *=bdp(sec ,fld)*

BDP retrieves a single value for a single security into a single Excel cell. The *sec* argument is the identifier, often the Bloomberg Ticker, of the particular security you are interested in and the *fld* argument is the particular property of the security you are interested in. The kind of data that Bloomberg and other data vendors supply is classified broadly into two main types; static data and real-time data. The former is data that tends to remain unchanged over time, for example the name of a company, or a bond's maturity date or its coupon rate. Real-time data is exactly that. It changes through the course of time depending on exactly when you look at it. Examples of real-time data would include currency exchange rates, the price of a stock and so on. The BDP function can access and return both real-time and static data fields. If you don't know the identifier of the security you are interested in you can use the various security lookup functions (e.g. TK, SRCH) from a Bloomberg terminal to help you. If you want to know which *flds* are available for you to use, click on the **Field Search** icon on the Bloomberg toolbar. Alternatively type in **FLDS <GO>** on a Bloomberg terminal to do the same thing. As a last resort you can always press the **Help** key twice on a Bloomberg terminal to consult with the Bloomberg Help desk.

If all this is confusing, a simple example will clarify things. Let us suppose we want to retrieve the latest bid price of, say, Microsoft. Before we can do this we need to gather a few bits of information to supply to our API function call. First of all we need to determine a security identifier for Microsoft. This can take many forms such as the Bloomberg Ticker or the ISIN. Various other identifiers can be used too but we will use the Ticker in our example. To determine what the ticker is we use the Bloomberg TK ticker lookup function from a Bloomberg terminal. Just type in **TK Microsoft** followed by the **<GO>** key and that will get you what you need to know. Doing this we can see that the Bloomberg ticker for Microsoft is in fact MSFT. We also have to tell Bloomberg what Market sector we are interested in getting the data from, bearing in mind that Microsoft related data will be present in both the equity and fixed income markets. If you have a Bloomberg keyboard you can see that the different market types are shown in the yellow function keys. We are interested in Microsoft's ordinary share price so the Market sector we need to use is Equity. If we *had* been interested in a Microsoft bond price we would have used the Corp market to indicate this. The one final piece of information we need to know is which property of the security we are interested in. We know it's the bid price but how do we know how to specify that to the Bloomberg API call. This is where the Bloomberg menu in Excel is invaluable. In this case the option we would take is Field Search then follow the on-screen instructions from there on. However I'll show a different way to do the same thing by using the Bloomberg terminal function **FLDS**. Just type in **FLDS <GO>** into the terminal. One of the fields that are shown will be Field Type. Ensure this is set to real-time only then type in the word *bid* into the search box followed by return. A list of possible hits will be returned and near the top you will see BID as being one of them. To confirm this is the correct choice you can click on it and Bloomberg will display a short description of what it is. We now have all the information we need so simply follow the steps below.

Start Excel and open a new worksheet, making sure of course that the Bloomberg Add In is available. Type the following text into cell A1,

=BDP("MSFT Equity","bid")

If all is OK you should see a number appearing in cell A1 which, assuming the US markets are open, frequently changes its value. This is the real-time bid price of Microsoft. It's as simple as that.

Looking at another example (see figure 2.2) let's say you are going on holiday to Europe and you want to find out what the latest cross rate is for the Euro versus USD. Go back into cell A1 and over type what's there with this

=BDP("EUR Curncy","bid")

Again you should see the bid price for the Euro versus USD appear in cell A1.

As the EUR is a currency, naturally the Bloomberg Market identifier we use this time is Curncy. In general, the securities and fields that your BDP functions process will more likely be contained in Excel cells rather than being typed in manually. So that, instead of having =BDP("EUR Curncy","bid") in cell A1 for instance, you would put the **EUR Curncy** and **BID** text into cells A1 and A2 for example and the formula **=BDP(A1,A2)** into cell A3.

figure 2.2

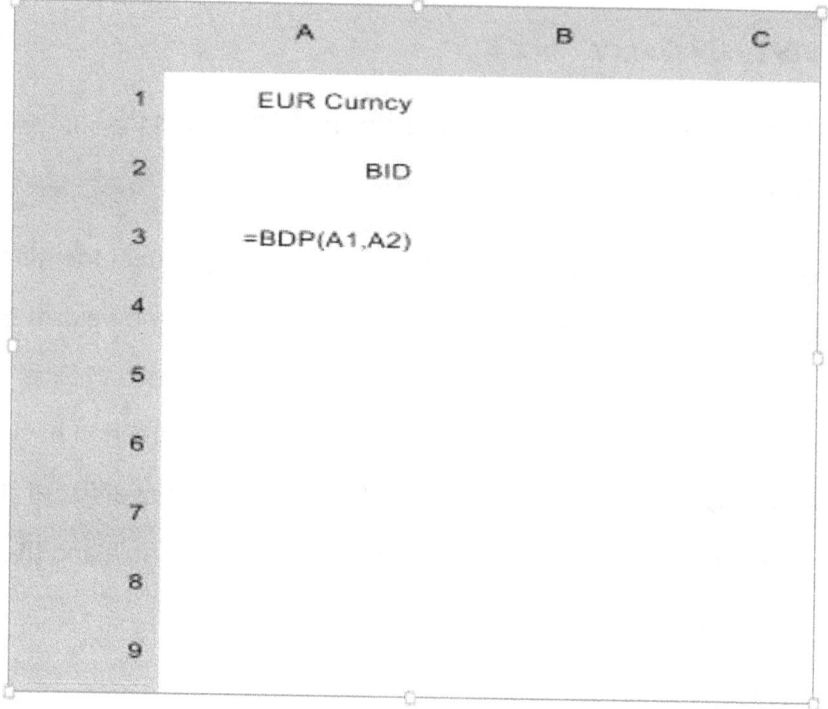

This way of doing it makes the process much more general. For instance if you now decided you wanted to retrieve the exchange rate for the Hong Kong dollar instead of the EURO you would simply overtype cell A1 with the appropriate currency ISO symbol, in this case HKD. Cell A3 would then start to show the new exchange rate for HKD instead.

The Bloomberg Data Set (BDS) Function

The syntax of this is **=bds(*sec, fld, other_optional_arguments*)**

The simplest BDS call has the same arguments as the BDP function. This time however the fld argument can - and usually will - return multiple data items into multiple Excel cells. Unlike BDP, BDS returns static data only. Again let's try a simple example (see figure 2.3) . Suppose we want to find out which securities make up the FTSE 100 index for example. The Bloomberg ticker - a kind of look-up code if you like - for the FTSE 100 is UKX and the field we want to use this time is INDX_MEMBER.

Start Excel and open a new worksheet and type the following into cell A1,

=BDS("UKX Index","INDX_MEMBER")

After hitting Return you ought to see a list of securities appear on column A of your spreadsheet starting at row 1 and going down to row 101. The first few lines are shown below. The LN part of each ticker name indicates that these shares are listed in London.

figure 2.3

	A	B	C	D	E
1	AAL LN				
2	ABF LN				
3	ADM LN				
4	ADN LN				
5	AGK LN				

NB. *The optional arguments of the BDS function need not concern us at this time but are used to enable you to do things like define the orientation of the result set – either vertical or horizontal -, the start column/row position in Excel you want the results to be displayed from, total number of rows to display and so on.*

The Bloomberg Data History (BDH) Function

The syntax of this is

=bdh(sec,fld,start_date,end_date,other_optional_arguments)

As you would expect this function call returns historical data between two different historical dates. Again, as with the BDS function, multiple data points will be returned to multiple cells within Excel. The call to BDH can only return static data. Let's look at an example. Start up Excel, open a new worksheet and type the following text into cell A1,

=BDH("MSFT Equity","last_price", "01-Jan-2012","01-Jun-1012")

This should result in the closing date and price for Microsoft being displayed starting at cell A1 between the dates we specified. The first few lines of output are shown below.

figure 2.4

	A	B	C
1	03/01/2012	26.765	
2	04/01/2012	27.4	
3	05/01/2012	27.68	
4	06/01/2012	28.105	
5	09/01/2012	27.74	
6	10/01/2012	27.84	

Using the API functions from VBA

Ok, now that we know a bit more about the Bloomberg Excel functions, the next step up from manually entering them into Excel is to do the same thing programmatically. This is what we'll look at now using the BDP function. As an example, let's say you have 30 different currencies that you want to track the cross rates of on a daily basis. Now you could enter this data manually and there would be nothing wrong in doing so but if you had to monitor 500 currency cross rates it would become a little tedious. I'll show two different scenarios. In the first I assume the 30 currencies, just the ISO codes, are contained in a simple text file called currencies.txt in the c:\ folder of your PC. In the second scenario I assume you have a database table called currency that contains a column called curr_iso that also contains all 30 ISO currency codes. The database I use is Oracle but the code is easily modified to use most modern database systems including MS Access, Sybase etc. All that should need changing is the ODBC connection string that you use. Ok, let's go. I'll just present the code and then go through some of the more interesting bits of it in more detail. For the sake of brevity, error checking is omitted for now.

listing 2.1

```
Sub get_bb_data()
    t = 1
    While cells(t, 1) <> ""
        Cells(t,2) = "=bdp("& CHR(34) & cells(t,1) & " Curncy" & _
        CHR(34) & "," & CHAR(34) & "bid" & _
```

```vba
        CHR(34) & ")"
        t = t + 1
    End While
End Sub
Sub get_currencies_from_database()
    Dim db_data As Connection
    Dim rs As Recordset
    db_data = New Connection
    rs = New Recordset
    ' If you have an appropriate Data Source Name (DSN), you
can
    ' use that instead of the TNS connect string
    ' methodology shown
    ' here which is Oracle specific
    ' Change the host IP, port number, database name,
    ' username and password appropriately
    db_data.Open "Driver={Microsoft ODBC for Oracle}; " & _
    "Server=(DESCRIPTION=(ADDRESS_LIST=" & _
    "(ADDRESS=(PROTOCOL=TCP)" & _
    "(HOST=127.0.0.1)(PORT=1521)))" & _
    "(CONNECT_DATA=(SID=oradb)));" & _
    "uid=myuid;pwd=mypass; "

    sqlstr = ""
```

```vba
    sqlstr = sqlstr & "select curr_iso  from currencies"

    rs.Open(sqlstr, db_data, adOpenStatic, adLockOptimistic)

    rs.MoveFirst()


    For t = 1 To rs.RecordCount

      Cells(t, 1) = rs.fields(0)

      rs.MoveNext()

    Next t

    rs.Close()

    db_data.Close()


End Sub


Sub get_currencies_from_text_file()

    ' arrays by default are zeroth based hence 29 rather than 30

    ' below in the DIM statement below

    Dim carray(29) As String

    Open "c:\currencies.csv" For Input As #1

    line = 0

    Do While Not EOF(1)

      Input #1, carray(line)

      carray(line) = carray(line)

      Cells(line + 1, 1) = carray(line)

      line = line + 1
```

```
    Loop
  Close #1
End Sub


Sub test()
        ' Use whichever of the below functions is relevant.
        ' Either way,  before the call to get_bb_data you want to
        ' end up with a list of your currencies in column A on
        ' your spreadsheet starting at
        ' cell A1 and going down to cell A30
        get_currencies_from_text_file()
        get_currencies_from_database()
        get_bb_data()
    End Sub
```

First off we want to read our list of currencies into column A of our spreadsheet. As mentioned earlier, often this list will either be contained in a simple text file or reside within some kind of database system. I've shown both methods of extraction. Use whichever applies to you. Remember, if extracting from a database to use your own connection string details. After we have gotten the currency codes into column A of our spreadsheet we need to construct our Bloomberg BDP API call for each of them. In this case it should look like:-

=BDP("XXX Curncy","bid")

where XXX is our 3 letter ISO currency code.

So we start at row 1 and loop around until we've exhausted our list of currencies, putting the results into column B. The CHR(34) function seen in the string concatenation is a way to represent the double quote (") character. The double quote character is ASCII 34. If you didn't use this you can always use 4 individual double quote characters to represent one double quote but I find this gets messy quite quickly so prefer to use CHR(34). That's all there is to it, after running the above code you ought to see the 30 currency exchange rates ticking over every so often in column B of your Excel sheet.

Downloading data using the COM data control

NB *The methodology discussed in this section has been superseded by an improved data control functionality which I discuss later, but I have kept it for those who might not have upgraded their Bloomberg in a while.*

The other main interface that Bloomberg exposes to programmers is the COM data control. This is Bloomberg's preferred way of interfacing its data with the likes of Excel/VBA or C++. Using the COM data control you can do everything you could do with the Excel API functions we have discussed above and much more besides. We'll take a quick look at it now to download a data set that we couldn't do using the EXCEL API functions – namely the cash flow of a bond. The cash flow of a bond tells   investors when they can expect the payment of their coupons, how much those coupon payments will be and also the final redemption payment i.e. normally the par value of the bond when it matures. It's also vital to know a bond's cash flow when calculating other bond analytics such as its yield-to-maturity, price and duration.

As usual I'll just show the code first then analyse it more fully afterwards.

listing 2.2

```
Dim vtresult As Object

Sub test()
    Dim secfields As Object
    Dim bbid_arr(500) As Object
    Dim xobj As BLP_DATA_CTRLLib.blpdata
    xobj = New blpdata
    arrayfields = Array("des_cash_flow", "coupon", "issue_dt",
"id_isin")

    Open "c:\bbids.csv" For Input As #1
    x = 0
    Do While Not EOF(1)
        bbid_arr(x) = ""
```

```vba
        Input #1, bbid_arr(x)

        bbid_arr(x) = bbid_arr(x) & " Corp"

        x = x + 1

    Loop

Close #1


xobj.subscribe(bbid_arr, x, arrayfields, Results:=vtresult)

nr_bonds = UBound(vtresult)


For I = 0 To nr_bonds

    coupon = vtresult(I, 1)

    issue_dt = vtresult(I, 2)

    isin = vtresult(I, 3)

    bbid = bbid_arr(I)

    For t = 0 To UBound(vtresult(I, 0))

        If t = 0 Then

            from_dt = issue_dt

        Else

            from_dt = vtresult(I, 0)(t - 1, 0)

        End If

        pay_dt = vtresult(I, 0)(t, 0)

        to_dt = pay_dt

        cashflow = vtresult(I, 0)(t, 1) / 10000

        Cells(t + 1 + tot, 1) = isin
```

```vba
        Cells(t + 1 + tot, 2) = bbid
        Cells(t + 1 + tot, 3) = from_dt
        Cells(t + 1 + tot, 4) = to_dt
        Cells(t + 1 + tot, 5) = pay_dt
        If coupon = 0 Then
            Cells(t + 1 + tot, 6) = 0
        Else
            Cells(t + 1 + tot, 6) = cashflow
        End If
        Cells(t + 1 + tot, 7) = coupon
        Cells(t + 1 + tot, 8) = "N"
    Next t
    Application.StatusBar = "Processing bond " & I + 1
    tot = tot + t
  Next I
  xobj = Nothing


End Sub
```

The first few lines of this code do a couple of very important tasks. First of all they reference the Bloomberg Data Control, secondly they set up an array *arrayfields* which tells the Data control which data/fields we want returned from Bloomberg and finally we assign a variant *vtresult* which will hold our returned data. I am assuming that there is a list of Bloomberg securities that we wish to obtain data for in the file c:\bbids.csv. This file should contain a single column of Bloomberg ID's. We open the file for reading and loop round the file and put our Bloomberg Id's into an array *bbid_arr*. So, by this stage we have two arrays, one containing the list of securities we want data for and the other containing the names of the data fields to retrieve. The next important step is the call the data control objects subscribe command. This is what actually fetches the data for us. We pass in the security ID array, the number of securities, the array of data items we want to retrieve and finally the variable which will hold our result set. After that it's simply a matter of looping around our result set and, in this case, outputting the results to our spreadsheet.

Downloading data using the new and improved data control

At my office we recently upgraded our PC to Windows 7 and Office 2013 and lo and behold the method shown above using **Subscribe** caused Excel to crash every time. I soon discovered that Bloomberg had - in fact quite some time ago - brought out a new data request/event driven model for downloading data. In short, you make a request for data and Bloomberg will asynchronously return the data to you as and when it becomes available - normally within seconds. Anyway, below is some code which does pretty much the same thing and the previous section did just to give you an example of what the new methodology looks like.

You'll need to ensure you have a reference in your VBA project to the Bloomberg API COM 3.5 Type Library before this code will work properly. Next, create a new regular module and put the following code into it.

listing 2.3

```vba
Public Sub RefData()
    Dim numSecurity As Integer
    Dim numFields As Integer
    t = 0
    numFields = 4
    Cells(1, 9) = 0
    Cells(1, 10) = ""
    Dim sSecurity() As String
    Dim Sec() As String
    Dim sFields() As Object
    ' the 100 below is arbitrary, make it as big as you need
initially
    ReDim sSecurity(0 To 100) As String
    ReDim sFields(0 To numFields - 1) As Variant


    'Delete any existing data that may be present
```

```vba
Columns("A:H").Select()

Selection.ClearContents()

' Our 4 fields as before

sFields(0) = "DES_CASH_FLOW"

sFields(1) = "COUPON"

sFields(2) = "ISSUE_DT"

sFields(3) = "ID_ISIN"

' Assume the BB ID's we want data for are in a file

x = 0

Open "e:\bbids.csv" For Input As #1

Do While Not EOF(1)

    sSecurity(x) = ""

    Input #1, sSecurity(x)

    If sSecurity(x) <> "" Then

        sSecurity(x) = sSecurity(x) & " Corp"

        x = x + 1

    End If


Loop

Close #1

ReDim Preserve sSecurity(0 To x - 1)


' Make the request for the data

bbControl.MakeRequest(sSecurity, sFields)
```

```
End Sub
```

Most of what the above code does is tell Bloomberg what fields and instruments that we are interested in getting data for. The real work of actually getting the data is done in the next section. So, now create a new class module named Data Control and put the following code into there.

listing 2.4

```
Option Explicit On

Private WithEvents session As blpapicomLib2.session
Dim refdataservice As blpapicomLib2.Service
' Instantiate the Bloomberg COM Control
Private Sub Class_Initialize()
    session = New blpapicomLib2.session
    session.Queue Events = True
    session.Start()
    session.OpenService("//blp/refdata")
    refdataservice = session.GetService("//blp/refdata")
End Sub
' Destroy the Bloomberg COM Control
Private Sub Class_Terminate()
    session = Nothing
```

```vba
End Sub


Public Sub MakeRequest(sSec List() As String, sFldList As Object)
    Dim req As Request
    Dim lRow As Long
    req = refdataservice.CreateRequest("ReferenceDataRequest")
    For nRow = LBound(sSecList, 1) To UBound(sSecList, 1)
        req.GetElement("securities").AppendValue(sSecList(nRow))
    Next
    For nRow = LBound(sFldList, 1) To UBound(sFldList, 1)
        req.GetElement("fields").AppendValue(sFldList(nRow))
    Next
    Dim cid As blpapicomLib2.CorrelationId
    cid = session.SendRequest(req)
End Sub
Private Sub session_ProcessEvent(ByVal obj As Object)
    Dim eventObj As blpapicomLib2.Event
    eventObj = obj
    Dim row As String
    Dim start_row As Integer
    On Error GoTo errHandler
    If Application.Ready Then
        If eventObj.EventType = PARTIAL_RESPONSE Or
            eventObj.EventType = RESPONSE Then
```

```vba
Dim it As blpapicomLib2.Message Iterator
it = eventObj.CreateMessage Iterator()
If Cells(1, 9) > 0 Then
    start_row = Cells(1, 9)
Else
    start_row = 1
End If
Do While it.Next()
    Dim i As Integer
    Dim msg As Message
    Dim numSecurities As Integer
    msg = it.Message
    numSecurities =
        msg.GetElement("securityData").NumValues
    For i = 0 To numSecurities - 1
        Dim security As Element
        ' BBID
        Set security =
msg.GetElement("securityData").GetValue(i)
        Dim fieldArray As Element
        fieldArray = security.GetElement("fieldData")
        Dim a As Integer
        Dim numfieldarray As Integer
        ' nr of fields, in our case this is 4
```

```vba
numfieldarray = fieldArray.NumElements

Dim des_cash As blpapicomLib2.Element

des_cash = fieldArray.GetElement(0)

Dim coup As blpapicomLib2.Element

coup = field Array.Get Element(1)

Dim iss_dt As blpapicomLib2.Element

iss_dt = field Array.Get Element(2)

Dim isin As blpapicomLib2.Element

isin = fieldArray.GetElement(3)

' nr of "records" returned by our bulk field

' des_cash_flow

Dim numBulkValues As Long

numBulkValues = des_cash.NumValues

Dim index As Long

Dim prev_date As String

prev_date = ""

' for each of our bulk field records, get each

' associated "element" and its value

For index = 0 To numBulkValues - 1

    Dim bulkElement As blpapicomLib2.Element

    bulkElement = des_cash.GetValue(index)

    Dim numBulkElements As Integer

    numBulkElements = bulkElement.NumElements

    Dim from_dt As String
```

```
Dim to_dt As String

Dim pay_dt As String

' Below info re: des_cash.datatype is for info only,

' we dont use it in this code

' des_cash.datatype=15 means its a compound field

' in this case the output of des_cash_flow

' this returns 3 fields , we only want the first two

Dim pdate As blpapicomLib2.Element

pdate = bulkElement.GetElement(0)

Dim amt As blpapicomLib2.Element

amt = bulkElement.GetElement(1)

If index = 0 Then

    from_dt = iss_dt.Value

Else

    from_dt = prev_date

End If

Cells(index + start_row, 1) = isin.Value

Cells(index + start_row, 2) =

    Left(security.GetElement("security").Value, 9)

Cells(index + start_row, 3) = from_dt

to_dt = pdate.Value

pay_dt = to_dt

Cells(index + start_row, 4) = to_dt

Cells(index + start_row, 5) = pay_dt
```

```
            If coup.Value = 0 Then

                Cells(index + start_row, 6) = 0

            Else

                Cells(index + start_row, 6) = amt.Value / 10000

            End If

            Cells(index + start_row, 7) = coup.Value

            Cells(index + start_row, 8) = "N"

            prev_date = pdate.Value

        Next index

     Next i

     Cells(1, 9) = index + start_row

     start_row = Cells(i, 9)

   Loop


   t = t + 1

   Cells(1, 10) = t & " Isins Processed/" & x & " Isins expected"

   If t = x Then

      MsgBox("Processing done")

   End If

  End If

 End If

Exit Sub


errHandler:
```

```
   Dim errmsg As Object

   errmsg = Err.Description

   Resume Next
End Sub
```

So, the above code should produce exactly the same output as the code in the previous section. Admittedly it's longer and slightly more complex but not by much. It's much more flexible though and due to the asynchronous nature of the calls now, it means your code can go and do other useful stuff while Bloomberg is working away in the background getting a hold of your data. You will also see that I have included some error checking code on the **session_ProcessEvent** module. It is important that all of your code includes some form of error checking. For VBA here is my simple but effective way of doing so.

listing 2.5

```
Private Sub my_module()

   On Error GoTo err_handler

   'All your main code goes below

   '

   ...
```

```vb
    ' Now the error handling bit

    ' These 2 lines will exit the sub

    ' after the error handler has been called

    '

endit:

    Exit Sub

    ' Finally the actual error handling code

    '

err_handler:

    MsgBox ( _

    "An unexpected error has been detected" & Chr(13) & _

    "Description is: " & Err.Number & ", " & Err.Description & _
Chr(13) & _

    "Module is: my_module" & Chr(13) & _

    "Please note the above details before contacting support")

    Resume endit

End Sub
```

It starts off by including the ON Error Goto err_handler line in the module or class you want error checking to happen in - this should be all of them of course! Next goes all your usual code that you want to run, followed by the label and line of code that exits your sub after the error handler has run and finally the error handler code itself. The beauty about doing it this way is that the error handling code is the same for every module with the exception of the *Module is:* part of the msgbox statement. It's simply a matter of cutting and pasting the same code to all your other modules. Easy and effective.

Before I leave the topic of the use of the Bloomberg terminal I just want to briefly discuss one more subject and that is the programmatic control of the Bloomberg desktop application itself via Dynamic Data Exchange which may be useful to some of you.

Controlling Bloomberg using DDE

I have to say that this is all a bit old hat now and it's not something that I've used very much and it's definitely not something that Bloomberg will provide support on if you experience issues with it but it may just prove useful in some cases. So, we will consider the following scenario. We assume that you are already logged into the Bloomberg terminal. So, you want to automate the following procedure.

Type in Microsoft's ticker and hit the <GO> function

Type in <DES> to bring up the description page for Microsoft

Print out the description page

We can do all of that in just five lines of code. Here's how.

listing 2.6

```
Dim ch as long

Ch = DDEInitiate("winblp","bbk")

Call DDEExecute(ch,"<blp-1><home>MSFT
US<EQUITY><GO>DES<GO>PRINT<GO>

Call DEDETerminat(ch)
```

The Bloomberg Data Licence Builder

My final topic on Bloomberg is on The Bloomberg data licence builder which is a separate stand-alone application to the Bloomberg terminal product. This was a new one on me until fairly recently but I think it's now one of Bloomberg's preferred ways of clients accessing Bloomberg data, particularly for large data sets. To my mind it's Bloomberg's riposte to Reuters Datascope Select product - which I discuss later on. Unlike the Reuters product the licence builder is not a web-based app but is one that you need to download from Bloomberg and run as a stand-alone application on a PC – normally the same PC that the Bloomberg terminal is installed on. You also need to obtain a separate username and password to log in to it. In use, briefly, you define a set of instruments you're interested in, a set of field data to return for those instruments and a job schedule for Bloomberg to retrieve that information. You then submit the data retrieval job and its output - when its run is complete - is stored on Bloomberg's server. The output, unless you specify otherwise, is encrypted. You can then FTP transfer the output file to your local server and process the data further as desired. The FTP transfer and decryption of the output file can be automated if   required and this is something you'll probably want to do.

Typically, once you log on to the application you are presented with 2 main screens. The first of these is called the **Request Builder (Options)** and it's this one that you use to build up a data retrieval job using familiar windows-like options such as drop-down lists, tick boxes etc. So, for instance, you would normally specify the output filename, pricing source, field delimiter and so on. You can then use the **Select** menu items to choose the desired instruments and data fields that you want to retrieve data for. If you want to automate the FTP transfer of an output file from the Bloomberg server to your local PC you can use the second screen which is called **Request Builder (FTP).** You can specify things like what time the FTP transfer is to happen at, whether or not to unzip the file if it's a zip or decrypt the output file as the transfer is happening. That last part is important as the application appears to encrypt any data it retrieves which is probably a good thing. One of the jobs I used the Data Licence Builder for was to download a couple of spot rates in the morning. The FTP transfer part wasn't automated so we ran a DOS batch job just after the time that the data retrieval job runs to get the data from the Bloomberg server to our PC. The code is shown below.

listing 2.7

```
echo on
rem
rem our file has todays date in YYYYMMDD format as its
extension                    rem
set mydate=%date:~-4,4%%date:~-7,2%%date:~-10,2%

set input_file=7amspots.%mydate%

set load_file=gm_fx7_load.txt
```

```
echo %mydate%

echo %input_file%

echo %load_file%

cd c:\blp\bbdl\rb5.0

del c:\gm\gm_fx7_load.txt

del %input_file%

rem

rem   The code below FTP's the data from the Bloomberg server
rem   to the  local PC and decrypts it at the same time

rem

c:\blp\bbdl\rb5.0\jre\bin\java -jar c:\blp\bbdl\rb5.0\bbdl.jar
-prog=ftp retrieve %input_file% label=GM_FTP autodecrypt

rem

rem check we got the file OK, error if not
rem

if not exist %input_file% goto no_input

copy %input_file% c:\gm\%load_file%

cd c:\gm
```

```
del gm_fx7.bad

del gm_fx7.log

del gm_fx7.out

if not exist %load_file% goto no_load

rem

rem   load the file into a staging table in the ORACLE database
rem

sqlldr myuser/mypass@mydb control=gm_fx7.ctl log=gm_fx7.log
bad=gm_fx7.bad

rem

rem check loading for errors
rem

if exist gm_fx7.bad goto badfile

rem

rem   final processing of the data from stage table to final table
rem

sqlplus myuser/mypass@mydb  @gm_fx.sql > gm_fx7.out

exit

:no_input
```

```
rem Send someone a message that there's a problem

msg mypcname "Error in currency download - no input file found
in c:\blp\bbdl\rb5.0\gm_fx7.yyyymmdd)

exit

:no_load

rem Send someone a message that there's a problem

msg mypcname "Error in currency download - no load file found
(c:\gm\gm_fx7.txt)

exit

:badfile

rem Send someone a message that there's a problem

msg mypcname "Error in currency sqlload - c:\gm\gm_fx7.bad file
found"

exit
```

The above code is pretty simple and well commented so I won't
discuss it in further but I think it's typical of the kind of automated
operation you'll want to do if using this product. I have to say I
didn't much like the Data Licence Builder when I first started using it

but it has definitely grown on me even though I still don't find it a particularly intuitive program to use.

Ok so that's me done with Bloomberg now. Time to turn our attention to that other financial data behemoth, Thomson Reuters.

3 DOWNLOADING FROM THOMSON REUTERS

When I first started writing this guide I was using Excel and Powerplus Pro and 3000 Xtra as my main interface to the data available on Thomson Reuters (I'm just going to call them Reuters from now on) and within that framework the main functions I used were RtGet and the Data Engine functions such as DEQuery, DEUpdate and a few others. However, that was then and since then Reuters have brought out an all new, all singing/all dancing product called Eikon which is their replacement for 3000 Xtra/Powerplus Pro and is a strategic product for them going forward. From what I can tell, the Data Engine functions and indeed RtGet have now been superseded by a new function called RData, although you can still use RtGet if you really want to. For those of you who are moving from Powerplus Pro to Eikon, Reuters provides a useful conversion tool that will translate all your old Excel's with their RtGets etc. and migrate them to the new way of doing things i.e. using RData. For the purposes of this guide though I am going to assume that you are coming to Reuters for the first time and that your interface will be Eikon and Excel.

Downloading data using Excel and the RDATA command

The first thing you need to be made aware of with Reuters is that all securities are tagged with the Reuters Identification Code – more commonly known as the RIC code. This is proprietary to Reuters in the same way that the Bloomberg Identifier is for Bloomberg and it's their way of identifying different securities on their system. If you want to get data out of Reuters, more often than not you will need one or more RIC codes. This can be a problem because quite often you won't know what the RIC code is. Perhaps the securities on your system will be tagged with the ISIN code for example. So a useful function is one that will retrieve the equivalent Reuters RIC code for one or more securities identified by their ISIN. This will be our first example. So open Excel and type the data into it as shown below.

figure 3.1

	A	B	C			
1	HK0000055209	=RDATA(A1:A2,"EJV.XFI.LISTRIC_1",,,,C1)				
2	HK0000055241					
3						

After you hit return in cell B1 you should see the following.

figure 3.2

	A	B	C				
1	HK0000055209	Updated	02Y1108 =CFIX				
2	HK0000055241		15Y2408 =CFIX				
3							

Cell B1 shows "Updated" which indicates that Reuters has finished its data retrieval and cells C1 and C2 ought to show the RIC codes associated with the ISIN codes in cells A1 and A2.

If we look closely at the RDATA command we can see that the first parameter is the range indicating where on the sheet our ISIN's are. The second parameter tells Reuters what data to return i.e. the RIC code and the final parameter tells Reuters where on the sheet to put the RIC codes it returns i.e. starting at cell C1. Don't get too hung up on the missing parameters. RDATA takes different parameters depending on what you ask it to do and I don't have room in this guide to go into details about what goes where and when. Suffice it to say that the online documentation for Reuters is exceptionally good and I would point you in that direction for more information if you need it. Just to round things off though let's add a bit more functionality to the above Excel sheet. As well as retrieve the RIC codes we will also get the price of the security. To do that we use the RDATA command again. Type the following command into cell D1

=RDATA(C1:C2,"PRIM ACT 1","RTFEED:IDN","FRQ:SNAP",,E1)

After the command has completed cell D1 should say Updated and cells E1 and E2 should contain the latest price of the two securities. If we look at the new RDATA command we can see that once again the first parameter is a reference to the position on the sheet where our securities of interest are, this time the two RIC codes we retrieved earlier. The second parameter tells Reuters what we want to retrieve, PRIM ACT 1 specifies the latest price. The third parameter tells Reuters which of its internal databases it should go to, to get the data. The fourth parameter indicates how often it should try and get the data, a one-time only snap in this case. And the final parameter indicates where on the sheet it should start to put the retrieved data, cell E1 in this case.

As in the case with Bloomberg all the above can also be done via VBA code too by simply assigning cells the various values we need at run-time.

Downloading data using The ADFIN analytic functions

One of the most powerful - and probably least used - methods Reuters provides for data access is called ADFIN. ADFIN is the umbrella term for the Reuters Financial Calculation Library of functions . There are literally hundreds of these functions and you really need to read the extensive HELP documents that Reuters provide on this and other topics but I am going to show you how to use one of them that I found personally very useful in my day job. The ADFIN method I will demonstrate is called DfListHolidays and this does the simple task of displaying holidays between two dates for a particular country. This can be very important in the finance world as   holidays affect accrual amounts, coupon payments, interest rates, time value of money issues, day count conventions etc. Without further ado here is my example. First of all you need to get the 3 letter code of the Market/Country you are interested in. This is usually the same as the ISO code but not always so. For instance for the UK its UKG which took me a long time to figure out. In our example we will try to determine the holidays in Argentina between the 1st January 2010 and the 31st December 2011. First of all we put the country code in cell A1, our start date range in cell A2 and our end date range in cell A3. So your spreadsheet should look like this:

figure 3.3

A	B	C	D	E	F	G	H	I	J	K	L	M	N	O	P
ARG															
01-Jan-10															
31-Dec-11															

Next we need to enter an array formula. First of all choose a suitable block of cells to put our returned data into. Since we will be returning both a date and the name of the holiday we need to choose two columns to put our data into. So, for example highlight cells B2 to C40. Next click on the formula bar and input the following formula:-

=DfListHolidays(A1,A2,A3,"RET:B150")

Hit CTRL-SHIFT-ENTER to turn this into an array formula (it will become surrounded by curly braces). Next hit RETURN and you ought to see something like that shown below.

figure 3.4

A	B	C
ARG	01/01/2010	New Year's Day
01-Jan-10	24/03/2010	Truth and Justice Memorial Day
31-Dec-11	01/04/2010	Holy Thursday
	02/04/2010	Malvinas Day
	01/05/2010	Labor Day
	25/05/2010	Anniversary of the Revolution
	20/06/2010	Flag Day

	09/07/2010	Independence Day
	16/08/2010	St. Martin's Day
	08/12/2010	Immaculate Conception
	25/12/2010	Christmas
	31/12/2010	New Year's Eve
	01/01/2011	New Year's Day
	07/03/2011	Carnival '11
	08/03/2011	Carnival '11

	24/03/201 1	Truth and Justice Memorial Day
	02/04/201 1	Malvinas Day
	21/04/201 1	Holy Thursday
	22/04/201 1	Good Friday
	01/05/201 1	Labor Day
	25/05/201 1	Anniversary of the Revolution
	20/06/201 1	Flag Day
	09/07/201 1	Independence Day

	15/08/201 1	St. Martin's Day
	10/10/201 1	Day of respect for cultural diversity'11
	08/12/201 1	Immaculate Conception
	25/12/201 1	Christmas
	30/12/201 1	1. New Year's Eve Observed
	31/12/201 1	New Year's Eve

As usual the above could be automated by way of VBA or just by using a whole series of hard-coded country codes across the sheet and equivalent dfListHoliday formulas. So, as you can see, nothing was particularly difficult there was it? The key is knowing about the dfListHoliday function as otherwise you'd be completely stumped. I urge you to check out the extensive documentation Reuters provides at its customer zone on this and other Reuters products, services and functions as I'm sure you will find plenty of other useful information there.

Downloading data in Reuters EIKON via screen scraping

Another data retrieval technique I have used quite a bit in Reuters is screen scraping. I used this a lot when trying to get currency exchange and forward rates that are supplied to Reuters from independent brokers such as BGC. It can be sometimes difficult to work out what the equivalent RIC's are for the data shown in these types of pages – sometimes there isn't one! So it's quite useful to be able to grab the whole page into Excel then post-process it, as it were, to get at the data you need. Let's look at an example. If on Eikon you type in the quote BGCNDΓ1, then assuming you have the correct permissions to view this data, you should see a screen similar to the following.

figure 3.5

```
Quote: BGCNDF1
Menu ▾  ↑ Q ▾ BGCNDF1          ● Search Related ▾ Trade ▾

13:48 16DEC13   BGC International            SP03725        BGCNDF1
21:48 SG TIME

     NEW TAIWAN DLR   KOREAN WON    INDIAN RUPEE   PHIL PESO    OUTRIGHT CNY
1D    FORWARD TWD     OUTRIGHT KRW  OUTRIGHT INR   OUTRIGHT PHP
SPOT 29.625/29.630   1052.4/1053.4  61.79/61.81   44.07/44.09  6.1095/6.1105
1WK  29.610/29.630   1052.9/1053.7  61.79/61.86   44.06/44.11  6.1110/6.1130
2WK                                                             6.1110 6.1130
3WK                                                             6.1110 6.1130

1MO  29.565/29.585   1053.8/1055.8  62.12/62.22   44.08/44.13  6.1110/6.1130
2MO  29.510/29.530   1055.5/1057.5  62.53/62.63   44.05/44.15  6.1120/6.1140
3MO  29.455/29.475   1057.2/1059.2  63.00/63.10   44.03/44.13  6.1120/6.1150
4MO
5MO
6MO  29.365/29.385   1061.8/1063.8  64.41/64.51   43.96/44.06  6.1160/6.1190
9MO  29.280/29.300   1065.4/1067.4  65.73/65.83   43.91/44.08  6.1215/6.1245
1YR  29.200/29.220   1068.8/1070.8  66.99/67.09   43.87/44.07  6.1280/6.1310
2YR                  1079.4/1084.4  70.90/71.40   43.50/43.80  6.1600/6.1800
3YR                  1082.9/1092.9                              6.2000/6.2200
4YR                                                             6.2400/6.2800
5YR                                                             6.2500/6.3000

SINGAPORE:  (65) 6510-2390        HONG KONG:  TOLL FREE 800 6510-2390
NEW YORK :  TOLL FREE 800 6510-2390   RICS:  <BGCSGRIC1>   INDEX:  <BGCSG>
```

So, say you were interested in the Taiwan 6 month forward bid and ask rates. That's the values shown as 29.365/29.385 about halfway down the above screenshot on the extreme left hand side. Go back to your Eikon and open up an Excel spreadsheet. Switch back to Eikon and left click your mouse with the pointer over the 29.365 figure referred to and drag the pointer into the Excel sheet. You should find that the whole 6 MO forward rates line shown above will magically appear on your Excel sheet. By clicking on it you will see the RDATA formula that Excel uses to get at this data. It will be something like

=RDATA("BGCNDF1","IRGROW 16","RTFEED:IDN","FRQ:2S",,J1)

Now that you have this, isolating just the BID and ASK of the Taiwan 6 month forward rate just requires a simple bit of string manipulation using the LEFT/RIGHT/MID VBA functions. Other rates within the same line can be scraped in the same way or indeed other lines retrieved by simply changing the value of the second parameter in the RDATA function.

Having gone through the above, I should point out there is a potential big problem using this methodology. You are effectively a hostage to the brokers who have been known to change around the position of prices on their pages. It doesn't happen that often but when it does it can really mess things up for you as you can imagine. If you possibly can and it not always is possible, which is why this technique can be useful – try to determine what the RIC code of the underlying security is. Once you have that you can simply use the RtGet (or RDATA) command instead.

Continuing this example, a search on Eikon quickly revealed that the RIC code for the 6 month TWD/USD forward rate is TWD6MNDFOR=BGCP. Since we've previously seen examples of the use of the RDATA command I thought it would be useful to use the older RtGet command instead. For our purposes RtGet takes three parameters. The first is the name of Reuters internal database it's using to look for our data. Just like in our RDATA examples we set to IDN. The second parameter is our RIC code and the third parameter is what data we wish to retrieve for our RIC – in this case we want the BID and ASK price. So, if you put the following into cells A1 and A2 of a blank excel sheet it should return the BID and ASK price of our forward currency.

=RtGet("IDN","TWD6MNDFOR=BGCP","BID") -> cell (A1) -> BID price of forward

=RtGet("IDN","TWD6MNDFOR=BGCP","ASK") -> cell (A2) -> ASk price of forward

Other Reuters Data Sources

Before leaving the subject of Reuters altogether I just want to quickly mention three other Reuters products that I've used. This is just to give you a very brief overview of them and make you aware that they exist as I don't have the space to go into much detail on them. You are more likely to come across these and/or use them if you need to access larger quantities of market data.

DATASCOPE SELECT

The first of the products is called Datascope Select (DSS for short). DSS is a web based front-end to Reuters market data which allows users to create and schedule data extracts and to bring those data extracts out in one of many different report formats. You will need a valid username and password before you can use it. Once you have logged in, to use DSS you need to supply a list of the instruments you are interested in. You do this by creating an Instrument List. This will normally be a list of RIC's or ISIN's or one of a number of other identifiers that can be typed in manually or imported from an existing file you have created one. After that you supply a list of the data items you want to retrieve for your list of instruments, what format each of the data items should be in and the overall format of the report including whether or not you want headers and footers added and its output format e.g CSV, XML. This is all done using the Report Template creation option. Once that's been done, it only remains for you to create a Schedule of when you want the data extract to be done. Simply supply the scheduler with your Instrument List and Report Template names, then tell it how often you want the extract to be run. This can be a one-off, daily, weekly or monthly task and can be at a specified time or simply when that data becomes available to Reuters. If you can, this is the product to use if you find yourself regularly having to download smallish market datasets. The next two products I talk about will definitely be of interest to you if your need is for much larger datasets.

DATASCOPE BULK EQUITY

With the Datascope Bulk Equity product the user gets access to more or less all of Reuter's equity data via a username/password protected FTP site. From a processing point of view it is much harder to deal with the data in this format than with the other formats we've discussed up until now and you really need to build a proper file extract and storage mechanism to get the most out of it. In my experience most users of this data will be mainly interested in the price and corporate actions data sets. In Datascope Bulk Equity, Reuters organises its data using the concept of file codes. An individual file code tends to represent a particular market e.g. file code 001 represents the Tokyo Stock Exchange as I recall. For each file code there will be a price file and a corporate actions file (plus correction and set–up/look-up files too). Additionally there are a series of historical files containing instrument data that allow you to prime your database so that you have a starting point for your daily process. Files are differentiated by their extension. For example .P for price files. The normal sequence of events would be to "prime" your database with static and historical data for the instruments you are interested in, then, on a daily basis, apply the price file data, then apply any correction data received. It is complicated by the fact that different data files become available at different times of the day due to their being file code (hence exchange) based which is why it can get quite tricky to set up a proper data extract mechanism under this system but it is definitely do-able.

REUTERS WORLDSCOPE

The most recent product I have had occasion to use is called Worldscope. This is a database of fundamental company data. By that I mean it's the type of data you would normally find on a company's published annual report. Some examples of the type of data items found in Worldscope would include your regular financial items like Earnings Per Share, Price to book ratios and so on but there are also more esoteric and harder-to-find items too. Interested in what the Natural gas production figures of an energy company are, or the average daily room rate of a hotel chain? You can find those in Worldscope and much, much more besides. In fact the data definition document alone for Worldscope comes in at a whopping 800 page PDF. Data items are provided using many different time-series frequencies but the most common are quarterly and annual. All financial data is provided in the currency of the domicile country.

Reuters makes their Worldscope data available via a password protected FTP site. Once per week (during the course of Monday) an updated, full database refresh is put on the FTP site and every day a series of change records is posted also. There are 50 files in total in zipped format, 20 zips representing US companies and 30 zips representing the rest of the world. You can elect to refresh your database every week and ignore intra-week changes, or you can prime your database once at the beginning and simply update it each day with the change records. Method 2 is more flexible and faster – once the initial database load is done - but harder to code. Method 1 is conceptually easier but takes an age to complete since the full database consists of approximately 100 million records. At the time of writing these records are spread out over 50 ZIP files each containing between 1 and 3 million records. 20 of the files contain data on US companies and the remaining 30 contain data on non-US companies. Out of the hundreds of data items available in the files it's likely you'll only be interested in a small subset of them so after getting the ZIP files and unzipping them you'll probably want to do a "grep" like command on them to isolate the records you're interested in before whatever other post-processing you want to do. If we assume that ultimately the data is going to be stored in a database, a **greatly** simplified sequence of operations for a weekly full refresh of the Worldscope data into your database might be something like:-

- connect to the Worldscope FTP site

- mget *.ZIP files for the latest date - > creates 50 .ZIP files onto your system

- unzip the zip files - > creates 50 .DAT text files on your system

- search the .DAT files for required data -> produces 50 .LOAD files

- truncate or delete down your existing Worldscope database table

- using your preferred bulk data loading tool, upload the 50 .LOAD files to your - newly emptied - Worldscope database table

4 Downloading from Markit

Markit is another of the big financial data vendors out there. It differs a bit in respect to Reuters and Bloomberg in that it is more focused on derivative market data. It's mechanisms for data retrieval are somewhat different too! Its preferred retrieval method is over the web and its preferred data format is XML. I have used three different ways to get data from Markit

Using cURL.

Hmm, how to best describe what cURL is? I guess it's like the son of a marriage between FTP and HTTP. Regardless of that, using cURL in my experience is a very reliable and quick way to access Markit's data. I think it's fair to say that cURL is Markit's preferred way of getting its users to access its data. If you don't have cURL on your system you can download a version for many different platforms at the cURL download page at https://curl.haxx.se/download.html. Below is an example of how to go about retrieving some Markit data via cURL. The dataset is for single name credit default swap (CDS) spreads. Substitute your own username and password in the command shown below.

```
$ curl --verbose --insecure --output cds_daily.zip --form
user=myusername -
```

--form password=mypassword --form date=20131216 --form format=CSV -

--form family="ITRAXX-EUROPE" --form report=COMPOSITES -

--form version=5 --form type=CDS
https://www.markit.com/export.jsp

What does this all mean? To be honest it doesn't really matter much. At the end of the day if you use this command (or similar) you will end up with a large zip file containing a large amount of CDS spread data. To see what this command is all about and what else is available please see the Markit XML guide (available at Markit's website). It's an excellent document and is one you should download and refer to when needed. I have also found that the support team (when you eventually get through to the right person) are also very good.

Via FTP.

This applies only to iBoxx data sets and is a hangover from Markit's takeover of iBoxx the index provider. iBoxx used FTP as its main delivery mechanism for data and Markit hasn't got around to switching it to its own way of doing things. Not much more to say on this. Get a login/password, connect to the FTP site and off you go!

Using Visual Basic

This is one of the most complex ways to get at Markit's data. Below is a sample piece of VB6 code that will get CDS fixed coupon data from Markit

listing 4.1

```
Option Explicit On
' Note: Enable the following in the References dialog box under
the Tools > '
' References menu in the VBA editor:
'OLE Automation' (to make a connection over the Internet)


Sub GetMarkitData()

    Dim doc 'As MSXML2.ServerXMLHTTP ' For storing the
downloaded report
    Dim s$  ' The string sent to the server for retrieving the report
    Dim filenumber#  ' For writing to the ZIP file
    Dim myfile  ' For iterating through the ZIP file
    Dim direc$

    Dim body1
    doc = CreateObject("msxml2.ServerXMLHTTP")
    doc.Open("POST", "https://www.Markit.com/export.jsp", False)
```

```
    doc.setRequestHeader("Content-Type",
"application/x-www-form-urlencoded")


    ' If you need to tell VB about your proxy server, you should
change
    ' ServerX-MLHTTP above to ServerXMLHTTP.4.0 or ....5.0
(depending on '
    ' your version of MSXML) and add:
    ' doc.setProxy 2, "proxy.bank.com:8080"    ' change me
    ' doc.setProxyCredentials "username", "password"    ' change
me
    ' Turn off SSL cert checking with this:
    ' doc.setOption 2, doc.getOption(2) -
    ' SXH_SERVER_CERT_IGNORE_ALL_SERVER_ERRORS
    ' The type parameter specifies either 'bond' or 'cds' instrument
type


    s = "user=" & "your_markit_username_goes_here" _
    & "&password=" & "your_markit_password_goes_here" _
    & "&version=" & "5" _
    & "&date=" & "20130109" _
    & "&format=" & "csv" _
    & "&report=" & "fixed_coupon" _
    & "&type=" & "cds"
```

```vba
' Send the request to the Markit website
doc.send(s)
' Handle the response

If (Left$(doc.responseText, 2) = "PK") Then ' A ZIP file has been
returned

    ' Save version=5 zip file to a directory
    ' requires WinZip or similar utility to be installed
    On Error Resume Next
    direc = "c:"
    On Error GoTo 0
    Dim inputFile() As Byte
    inputFile = doc.responseBody
    filenumber = FreeFile
    Dim body2() As Byte
    body1 = doc.responseBody
    ReDim body2(UBound(body1))
    body2 = body1
    Open direc & "\file.zip" For Binary Access Write As
#filenumber
    Put #filenumber, 1, inputFile
    Close #filenumber
```

```
    doc = Nothing


    ' By this stage you should have a zip file available
    ' so you could do something like use winzip to unzip it
    Shell("""c:\program files\winzip\winzip32.exe""" -e -o """ &
direc & "\file.zip""""" & direc & """")
      ' -e extract
      ' -o overwrite
      ' Give winzip time to do its stuff


      Application.Wait(Now + TimeValue("0:00:5"))
      ' By this stage your CSV file should be available for you to
further process or what-ever
    Else
      ' oops something didnt work right
      MsgBox("No zip file returned, please investigate")
    End If


End Sub
```

Accurate and up to date market data has started to become available from a number of Internet sites in recent years. This important and growing new source of data is easily tapped into by ordinary users with the aid of some simple Excel/VBA programs. Oftentimes you don't even need to code anything but can simply click on a link or type in a URL to get at the data. And unlike most data vendors we've discussed so far, the data here is (mostly) free. The flip side of this of course is that the data is probably not quite as accurate, up-to-date or comprehensive either. Anyway, three of the most important of these sites are Google Finance, Yahoo Finance and Quandl and I'll show worked examples of getting data from both of those websites. I also mention a useful website that you can download historical FOREX tick data from without needing any coding at all. Finally, there is a small section on general web-scraping techniques you can implement relatively easily in code.

Google Finance

Google finance was launched by Google in the mid 2000's and is now a huge repository of financial information including, but not limited to, stock prices, market news, industry trends and market index levels. It also boats a stock screener and portfolio construction tool which can be used to monitor your personal finances.

Downloading from Google Finance via Excel's Web Query

In case you didn't know, Excel has a useful built in tool that enables you to grab data from most websites quite easily and without any programming code at all. It's called the web query and works like this. Let's say we want to get the latest GBP/USD currency exchange rate. We can see that on google, the page to go to is

http://www.google.com/finance?q=GBPUSD&ei=qxyvUrjnD4m30AH 87AE

This should bring up a page on your browser like:-

figure 5.1

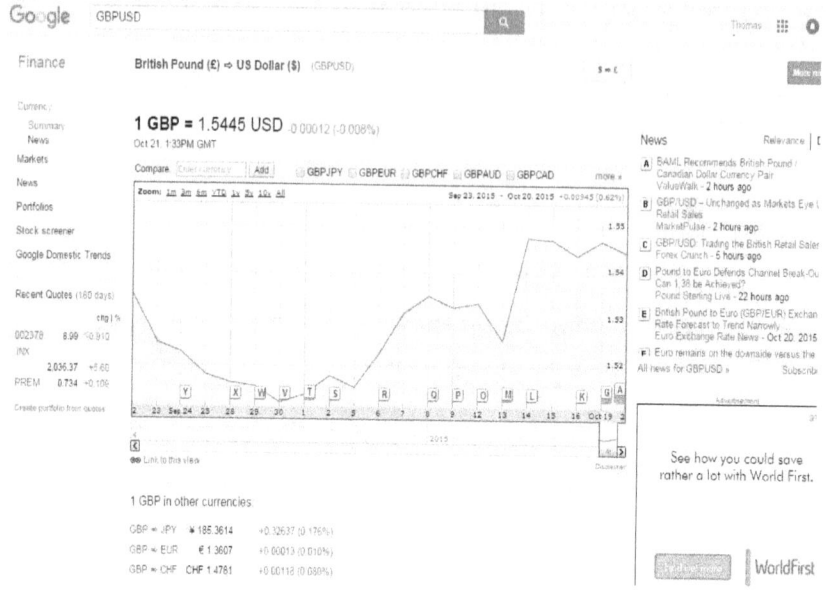

The data we want to get our hands on is the 1 GBP = 1.5445 USD bit near the top of the page. First of all open Excel and under the Data menu item you should see a From Web icon. Click this and a kind of mini browser will appear on screen. Type the address http://www.google.com/finance?q=GBPUSD&ei=qxyvUrjnD4m30AH 87AE into the address bar and the Google finance website should appear with our GBP/USD rate prominent near the top of the page. Simply click on the little yellow arrow next to the table you want to import into Excel. The arrow will turn into a little green tick mark. At this stage you can just click on the import button. You will receive a prompt asking you to enter which cell you want the import to start at. The default of cell $A$1 is fine for us. So now you should see the data in the spreadsheet. When I did the above the GBP/USD rate appeared at record number 50 on my spreadsheet.

The data is pretty unstructured I know but if you wanted to you could write some VBA code to automate tidying it up a bit. The other good thing is that you can record all the keystrokes you did to get to this point and create a macro which means this task can be fully automated going forward.

Yahoo Finance

Much like Google did a year earlier , in 2007 Yahoo decided to launch its own financial web-site, pretty much mimicking most of what Google had done with theirs. Also like Google, the data you're most likely to want to see is kind of buried deep in their web pages and depends on you knowing the right URL to use.

DOWNLOADING DATA FROM YAHOO FINANCE

The secret to getting data from Yahoo finance is in the URL you supply to it. One of the commonest formats is shown below.

http://finance.yahoo.com/d/quotes.csv?s= *symbols&f=flags*

Where **symbols** is a + separated list of company tickers and **flags** that tells yahoo what data you want to return for each company. A list of the common flags are shown below.

figure 5.2

a	Ask	a2	Average Daily Volume	a5	Ask Size
b	Bid	b2	Ask (Real-time)	b3	Bid (Real-time)
b4	Book Value	b6	Bid Size	c	Change & Percent Change
c1	Change	c3	Commission	c6	Change (Real-time)

c8	After Hours Change (Real-time)	d	Dividend/Share	d1	Last Trade Date
d2	Trade Date	e	Earnings/Share	e1	Error Indication (returned for symbol changed / invalid)
e7	EPS Estimate Current Year	e8	EPS Estimate Next Year	e9	EPS Estimate Next Quarter
f6	Float Shares	g	Day's Low	h	Day's High
j	52-week Low	k	52-week High	g1	Holdings Gain Percent
g3	Annualized Gain	g4	Holdings Gain	g5	Holdings Gain Percent (Real-time)
g6	Holdings Gain (Real-time)	i	More Info	i5	Order Book (Real-time)
j1	Market Capitalization	j3	Market Cap (Real-time)	j4	EBITDA
j5	Change From 52-week Low	j6	Percent Change From 52-week Low	k1	Last Trade (Real-time) With Time
k2	Change Percent (Real-time)	k3	Last Trade Size	k4	Change From 52-week High

k5	Percent Change From 52-week High	l	Last Trade (With Time)	l1	Last Trade (Price Only)
l2	High Limit	l3	Low Limit	m	Day's Range
m2	Day's Range (Real-time)	m3	50-day Moving Average	m4	200-day Moving Average
m5	Change From 200-day Moving Average	m6	Percent Change From 200-day Moving Average	m7	Change From 50-day Moving Average
m8	Percent Change From 50-day Moving Average	n	Name	n4	Notes
o	Open	p	Previous Close	p1	Price Paid
p2	Change in Percent	p5	Price/Sales	p6	Price/Book
q	Ex-Dividend Date	r	P/E Ratio	r1	Dividend Pay Date
r2	P/E Ratio (Real-time)	r5	PEG Ratio	r6	Price/EPS Estimate Current Year
r7	Price/EPS Estimate Next Year	s	Symbol	s1	Shares Owned
s7	Short Ratio	t1	Last Trade Time	t6	Trade Links
t7	Ticker Trend	t8	1 yr Target Price	v	Volume

v1	Holdings Value	v7	Holdings Value (Real-time)	w	52-week Range
w1	Day's Value Change	w4	Day's Value Change (Real-time)	x	Stock Exchange
y	Dividend Yield	s2	shares outstanding		

For example let's say we wish to get the bid and ask price of Microsoft and Yahoo. The company symbols we need are MSFT for Microsoft and YHOO for Yahoo itself. From the above table we can see that the flags we need to provide are **b** for bid and **a** for ask. We'll also supply the flag **s** for the symbol so we can tell which data goes with which quote. So if we typed in the following to a web browser and downloaded the data into Excel

http://download.finance.yahoo.com/d/quotes.csv?s=YHOO+MSFT&f=sba

We should get back a sheet that looks something like:

figure 5.3

	A	B	C	D	E	F	G	H	I
1	YHOO	30.71	30.72						
2	MSFT	46.95	46.96						
3									
4									
5									
6									
7									
8									
9									
10									
11									
12									
13									
14									
15									
16									
17									
18									

Another common task is to get historical price data for one or more securities. Again using the proper URL is the key to this. Below is one of the commonest requests which returns the historical price date, open, high, low, close, volume and adjusted close for a particular stock (in this case Yahoo) between the dates of 1ˢᵗ Jan 1995 and the 13th Dec 2013.

http://ichart.finance.yahoo.com/table.csv?s=YHOO&a=0&b=1&c=1995&d=11&e=16&f=2013&g=D&ignore=.csv

This will create a CSV file called table.csv and optionally open it within Excel.

AUTOMATING THE LOADING OF FINANCE DATA FROM YAHOO INTO EXCEL

Here is a short example of loading financial data from Yahoo into Excel. This example is just a simple stock screener. The idea is that you supply a list of stock tickers that you want to monitor and at the click of a button the program will retrieve basic price information and display it on the spreadsheet. We'll logically split our sheet into two parts. The top half will be our portfolio of stocks we're actually invested in and the bottom half will be our universe of stocks that we are either already invested in or might want to be invested in in the future. The data in our portfolio will be derived from the data in our universe of stocks - data that we download from Yahoo. In my example I'm using Oil & Gas and mining stocks that are listed on London's AIM market.

figure 5.4

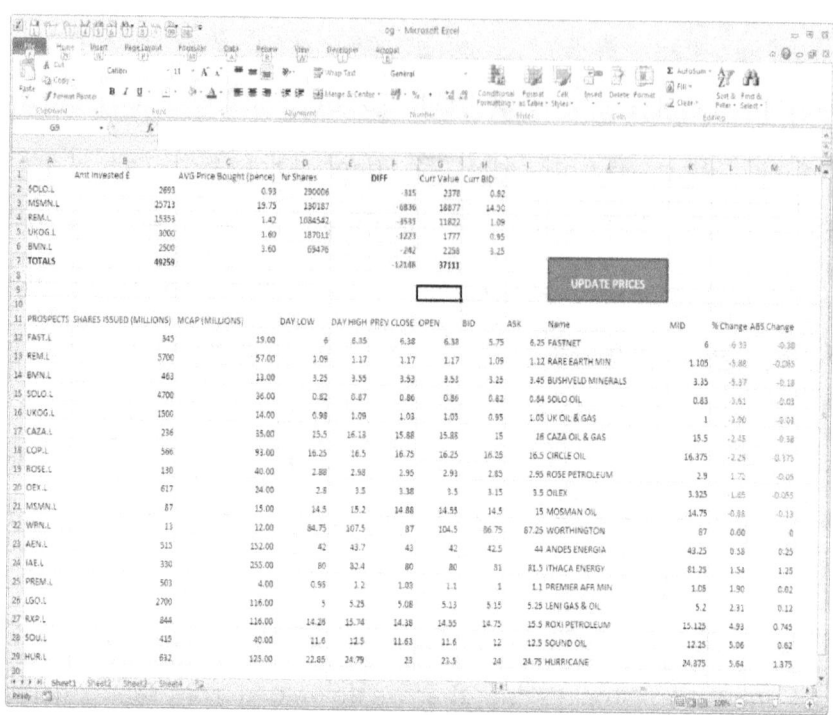

So, the tickers of my portfolio are in cells A2 to A6. The amounts invested, average purchase price and number of shares purchased in cells B2 to D6 are all just plain hard-coded text. The data in cells F2 to H6 are just formulas.

e.g

Cell F2 (difference between current value of stock and amount invested) = "**=G2-B2**" and is then copied down to cell F6.

Cell G2 (current value of stock) = "**=D2*H2/100**" and is then copied down to G6

Cell H2 (current BID price of the stock) = **"=INDIRECT("H" &**

MATCH($A2,$A$12:$A$54,0)+11)" and is then copied down to cell

H6. Cells F7 and G7 are just **SUMS** of the cells above them.

Now onto our list (universe) of prospective stocks. Again cells A12 to

C29 are just hard-coded text values. Cells A12 to A29 just contains

the list of stock tickers we want to retrieve data for. For

convenience I've hard-coded the shares in issue and market cap into

columns B and C but you could retrieve this data from Yahoo if you

wanted. The important part is the code behind the Update button.

Pressing this will update cells D12 to J29 with data downloaded

from Yahoo. Cells K12 to K29 contain a formula which derives the

MID price and cells L12 to L29 contain a formula to derive the

percentage change between the current MID price and the previous

CLOSE price. The code for this is shown below.

listing 5.1

```
Sub test()
    t = 12 ' start row of the universe of prospective stocks
    Range("d12", "J29").Select()
    Selection.Clear()
    While (Cells(t, 1) <> "")
        qURL =
"http://download.finance.yahoo.com/d/quotes.csv?s=" & Cells(t,
1) &
```

```vba
            "&f=ghpobanp"
    http = CreateObject("MSXML2.XMLHTTP")
    http.Open("GET", qURL, False)
    http.Send()
    pstr = Split(http.responseText, ",")
    Cells(t, 4) = Format(pstr(0), "#0.00")
    Cells(t, 5) = Format(pstr(1), "#0.00")
    Cells(t, 6) = Format(pstr(2), "#0.00")
    Cells(t, 7) = Format(pstr(3), "#0.00")
    Cells(t, 8) = Format(pstr(4), "#0.00")
    Cells(t, 9) = Format(pstr(5), "#0.00")
    Cells(t, 10) = Replace(pstr(6), """", "")
    http = Nothing
    t = t + 1
  End While
  Macro1()
End Sub


' This is just to sort our data
Sub Macro1()
  Range("A12:M29").Select()
  ActiveWorkbook.Worksheets("Sheet1").Sort.SortFields.Clear()
  ActiveWorkbook.Worksheets("Sheet1").Sort.Sort
```

```
    Fields.Add(Key:=Range("L12:L29") _
    , SortOn:=xlSortOnValues, Order:=xlAscending,
DataOption:=xlSortNormal)
    ActiveWorkbook.Worksheets("Sheet1").Sort.Sort
    Fields.Add(Key:=Range("B12:B29") _
    , SortOn:=xlSortOnValues, Order:=xlAscending,
DataOption:=xlSortNormal)

    With ActiveWorkbook.Worksheets("Sheet1").Sort
        .SetRange Range("A11:M29")
        .Header = xlYes
        .MatchCase = False
        .Orientation = xlTopToBottom
        .SortMethod = xlPinYin
        .Apply()
    End With
End Sub
```

Quandl

Quandl - https://www.quandl.com - is a relative newcomer to the world of financial data provision. It aggregates data sets from many different sources and makes searching for the data fairly easy. It has interfaces to the popular languages R and Python as well as to Excel and you can also download in various formats such as JSON, XML and CSV via calls to cURL. You can even just type in an appropriate API call directly into your browser to initiate a download of data.

NB If you don't have cURL on your system you can download a version for many different platforms from the cURL download page at https://curl.haxx.se/download.html.

DOWNLOADING DATA FROM QUANDL USING ITS API

A large percentage of the data available on Quandl is totally free but there are some restricted - so called premium datasets - which require a subscription in order for you to access them. The data on Quandl is subdivided into databases with each database covering a single subject such as end of data stock prices, global economic indicators and so on. Within each database you can access the entire database via the databases API, a two dimensional array subset of the database via the datatables API or a time-series cut of the database via the datasets API. You can download a list of all available databases by typing the following URL into your browser :-

https://www.quandl.com/api/v3/databases.csv?api_key=YOURKEY HERE

There is also a special unrestricted database called WIKI which contains end of day stock prices, dividends and splits for over 3,000 US companies. That's the general gist of what Quandl is about. Before looking at some examples you should visit the Quandl web page and register. Unregistered users are subject to a limit of 50 downloads per day and indeed this is expected to be deprecated at some point in the future. Registered users are allowed 2000 calls to the database per 10 minutes subject to a maximum of 50000 calls per day. Registering is free and easy and well worth doing. When you register you will be given a unique API key which is used in all the calls you make to the database to indicate that you are registered correctly. The following are all examples of using the Quandl API, that is to say, you just type in a URL into your web browser to initiate a download of data, there is no need to download any additional software.

Download a list of available databases

https://www.quandl.com/api/v3/databases.xml?api_key=YOURKEYHERE

Get data about a database

For example typing the following URL into your browser

https://www.quandl.com/api/v3/databases/WIKI.xml?api_key=YOURKEYHERE

should return a response similar to:-

```
<quandl-response>

  <database>

    <id type="integer">4922</id>

    <name>Wiki EOD Stock Prices</name>

    <database-code>WIKI</database-code>

    <description>

      End of day stock prices, dividends and splits for 3,000 US
      companies, curated by the Quandl community and released
      into the public domain.

    </description>

    <datasets-count type="integer">3180</datasets-count>

    <downloads type="integer">442538309</downloads>

    <premium type="boolean">false</premium>

    <image>
```

https://quandl-data-upload.s3.amazonaws.com/uploads/so
urce/profile_image/4922/thumb_thumb_quandl-open-data-
logo.jpg

</image>

<favorite type="boolean">false</favorite>

</database>

</quandl-response>

Get a historical time-series of a stock's price from the WIKI database

To initiate a download of , say, historical daily end of day open, high, low, close and volume, dividends and splits, and split/dividend adjusted open, high, low close and volume for Apple, just type the following URL into your web browser:-

https://www.quandl.com/api/v3/datasets/WIKI/AAPL.xml?api_key=Y
OURKEYHERE

If you wanted a CSV file instead just change the .xml at the end of the URL to be .csv

There are various other options that allow you to customise the time-series data that you get from returned datasets. Among the most common are the ability to change the periods returned via the **collapse** keyword, the ordering of the dataset via the **order** keyword, filtering which columns are returned via the

column_index keyword and restricting the number of rows returned via the **rows** or **start_date/end_date** keywords. More information on these and other topics can be found on the Quandl web-site.

DOWNLOADING DATA FROM QUANDL USING R

I've recently discovered the programming language R and was quite intrigued by its sophisticated statistical, graphics and data handling capabilities so I thought I'd write a bit about accessing Quandl data using it. R is a free software environment and compiles and runs on a wide variety of UNIX platforms, Windows and MacOS. You can download R at The Comprehensive R Archive Network known as CRAN - https://cran.r-project.org/

To demonstrate how easy it is to get and display Quandl datasets in R for our first R program we are going to download and plot a line graph of the daily closing price of Apple's stock. First of all we need to know which database and ticker to use. For Apple we will use the EOD (end-of-day) database and Apple's identifier within that database is AAPL. The program itself is very short and is shown below along with its graphical output. Please note that the line numbers shown in the code listing are for display purposes only and are not part of what you would type into the R code window.

listing 5.2

```
1  install.packages("Quandl")
2  install.packages("ggplot2")
3  library(Quandl)
4  library(ggplot2)
5  Quandl.api_key("YOURKEYGOESHERE")
6  stock_aapl <-
Quandl("EOD/AAPL",start_date="2013-01-01")[,c("Date","Close"
)]
7  ggplot(stock_aapl,aes(x=Date)) +
geom_line(aes(y=Close),color="red")
```

Running the above code in R will result in a graph similar to the one shown below.

figure 5.5

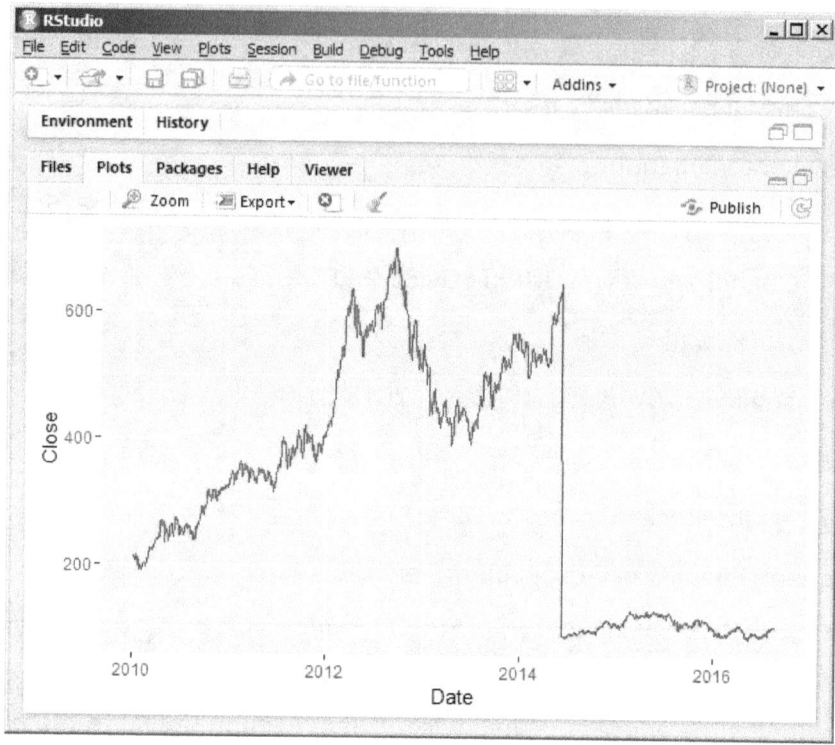

Incidentally, the big apparent drop in the price in the middle of 2014 was caused by a 7 for 1 stock split. If we look at the code listing again, although the syntax might be unfamiliar, I'm hoping you get the general idea of what it's doing.

Lines 1 - 2

We have two install commands which do what you'd expect in that they make available to R packages which contain enhanced connectivity and utilities outside its core functionality. In this respect they are much like a JAVA import or C #include directive for those of you familiar with those languages.

Lines 3 - 4

The library keyword attaches the contents of the packages to the current run-time R environment.

Line 5

This is where you tell Quandl what your API key is. Obviously you would substitute your own actual key value for the placeholder value shown in the listing.

Line 6

This is the actual call to get the stock price data from Quandl. We pass in the database/ticker symbol which uniquely identifies the stock to Quandl, we state that we want the data to start on the 1st January 2013. Since we don't specify an end date we will get everything from the start date onwards. The final **'c'** parameter tells Quandl that we only want certain **(c)**olumns returned - namely the Date and Close price. We assign the whole data set that's returned to a variable called stock_aapl. If at this stage we had simply printed out this variable by typing show(stock_aapl) into R we just see two columns of data displayed. With data like this though it's preferable to see a graph of it which is what the final line of code does.

Line 7

This is where we plot the close price against the date. We are using a popular graphics package called ggplot2 and to be honest whole books have been written just about graphing in R with ggplot2 so if you want to know more please consult those or one of the many online tutorials. My brief explanation is that we pass in to ggplot2 our variable holding the data set - stock_aapl. We then specify what ggplot2 calls an an (**aes**)thetic - basically what we want the x -axis to be, a (**geom**)etric type i.e a line graph, followed by two final parameters associated with the line graph. Another aesthetic, this time a specification of the y axis and finally what colour we want the line graph to be - red.

To round off our discussion of R here is a final program showing how we can use it to compute some useful analytics on our downloaded data set of Apple stock prices. We will use the example of calculating the price volatility. You may recall that the volatility of a stock's price is the annualised standard deviation of its price returns, so let's write a little R program that calculates this for us.

listing 5.3

```
1  library(Quandl)
2  stock_aapl
<-Quandl("WIKI/AAPL",start_date="2013-01-01",end_date="201
4-01-01")
3  aapl_close <- stock_aapl$Close
```

```
4  n <- length(aapl_close)
5  dly_ret <- log(aapl_close[-n]/aapl_close[-1])
6  vol <-sd(dly_ret)*sqrt(252)
```

Line 1

We make the Quandl datasets available to R

Line 2

We fetch 1 years worth of data. Note that we don't need to specify the API key in this instance as we are using the free WIKI Quandl database.

Line 3

Our fetch in line 2 will get a whole bunch of price related data - not just the close price, so this line stores just the closing price into an array variable.

LIne 4

We store the number of data points we have retrieved.

Line 5

We calculate and store the compounded daily price returns. To explain, in R if we have an array of n values x, then x[-n] will return an array of those values minus the last value and x[-1] will return an array of values except the first. So for example let's say our array of daily returns x is [1,2,3,4,5]. x[-5] will be [1,2,3,4] and x[-1] will be [2,3,4,5], so x[-5]/x[-1] will result in the array [1/2 , 2/3 , 3/4 , 4/5] which is what we want.

Line 6

This is just our calculation of the volatility, sd is the standard deviation of the daily returns and we multiply to get the annualised volatility.

To sum up, although R may not be the most intuitive language to follow, I have hopefully whetted your appetite to encourage you to find out more about it. Seven lines of code to retrieve the price history of a stock and to plot that history on a line graph is pretty impressive.

A useful web-site for intra-day historical FOREX tick data

Recently I was wanting to do some analysis on historical intraday foreign exchange (FOREX) data and was struggling to find a source of large and free datasets. Eventually I was directed to a useful site that provides minute-by-minute historical tick data for around fifty of the commonest currency pairings. The home page of this web-site is http://www.forexite.com but the actual data is buried deep within the pages of this site. The secret to getting at the data is in the URL you type into your browser. What you must do is type in the full URL as shown below

http://www.forexite.com/free_forex_quotes/YYYY/MM/DDMMYY.zip

You need to replace the Y, M and D's shown in the above URL with the required four or two digit year, the two digit month and the two digit day of the month that you want the data for. As an example suppose you want the 1 minute intra-day tick data for the 1st November 2011. The URL you would type into your browser is:-

http://www.forexite.com/free_forex_quotes/2011/11/011111.zip

When you do this you ought to see that a zip download starts immediately from your browser. Once the download has finished you can open up the zip archive and it should contain one text file with the same name as the ZIP but with a.txt extension. This text file is comma separated which means it's really easy to import it into excel for further analysis.

Getting data using general web scraping techniques

Often you'll come across a website that shows some useful data on its page that you'd like to grab and import, say, into Excel. Depending on how the particular data is rendered on the web page it's reasonably straightforward to grab it for yourself. The first thing to check is how the data is rendered on the page. For that you need to examine the page source. On most browsers there is an option to do this. For instance under Chrome and Internet Explorer you simply right click on the web page and take the View Source option that displays in the mini menu that pops up. Now look at the source data and see if you can pick out from that the data you are interested in. If you can then you ought to be able to grab it using VBA. For this example I will consider a simple test page that I set up on GitHub pages. You can see the page by following the link to https://taupirho.github.io/stock_prices. The page is shown below and, as you can see, it's just a list of ten dummy stocks, showing their name, price, price date and volume of shares traded on the price date.

figure 5.6

A table showing some sample stock data

Stock Name	Price	Price Date	Volume
Stock A	12.90	01-Apr-2017	234,000
Stock B	0.09	24-Mar-2017	10000
Stock C	89.0	30-Ap-2016	1900333
Stock D	3.44	01-Oct-2011	984556
Stock E	104.89	01-Dec-2012	7422
Stock F	23.66	01-Apr-2017	295558
Stock G	34444	10-Jun-2013	5778
Stock H	100.00	20-May-2013	33
Stock I	33.34	05-May-2013	8474754
Stock J	12.90	16-Sep-1999	64929

So let's say we wanted to capture this information and display it in Excel. The first thing to do is to right click the web page and view the HTML source. Now, look at the HTML code and see if we can find the price date, name and volume there. In fact we can and here is a snippet of the relevant section.

```
<table>

    <thead>

    <tr>

    <th>Stock Name</th>

    <th>Price</th>

    <th>Price Date</th>

    <th>Volume</th>

    </tr>

    </thead>

    <tbody>

    <tr>

    <td>Stock A</td>

    <td>12.90</td>

    <td>01-Apr-2017</td>

    <td>234,000</td>

    </tr>

    <tr>

    <td>Stock B</td>

    <td>0.09</td>

    <td>24-Mar-2017</td>

    <td>10000</td>
```

```
</tr>

<tr>

<td>Stock C</td>

<td>89.0</td>

<td>30-Ap-2016</td>

<td>1900333</td>

</tr>

<tr>

<td>Stock D</td>

<td>3.44</td>

<td>01-Oct-2011</td>

<td>984556</td>

</tr>

<tr>

<td>Stock E</td>

<td>104.89</td>

<td>01-Dec-2012</td>

<td>7422</td>

</tr>

<tr>

<td>Stock F</td>
```

```html
<td>23.66</td>

<td>01-Apr-2017</td>

<td>295558</td>

</tr>

<tr>

<td>Stock G</td>

<td>34444</td>

<td>10-Jun-2013</td>

<td>5778</td>

</tr>

<tr>

<td>Stock H</td>

<td>100.00</td>

<td>20-May-2013</td>

<td>33</td>

</tr>

<tr>

<td>Stock I</td>

<td>33.34</td>

<td>05-May-2013</td>

<td>8474754</td>
```

```
</tr>

<tr>

<td>Stock J</td>

<td>12.90</td>

<td>16-Sep-1999</td>

<td>64929</td>

</tr>

</tbody>

</table>
```

Let's say you wanted to scrape this page for the volume figure associated with the stock called Stock D for example. Basically what we have to do is search through the source of the web page for the string "Stock D" then do a bit of text manipulation to get at the value we need. There are a number of ways you can get to the volume value from there but, looking at the source code of the web page, what I would do is this. From the string "Stock D" read forward for the next three strings of the form "<td>". Once you've done that you should be at the start of the volume figure and then just keep reading data up until the next "</td>" string. It sounds a bit more complicated than it actually is.

Below is an example of the type of code we would need.

listing 5.4

```vba
Sub getwebdata()
    Dim xmlhttp As Object
    Dim strURL As String
    Dim CompanyID As String
    Dim websource As String
    Dim sSearch As String


    strURL = "https://taupirho.github.io/stock_prices/"
    Set xmlhttp = CreateObject("msxml2.xmlhttp")
    With xmlhttp
        .Open "get", strURL, False
        .send
        websource = .responsetext
    End With
    findstr1 = "Stock D"
    findstr2 = "<td>"
    findstr3 = "</td>"


    i1 = InStr(1, websource, findstr1)
    substr1 = Mid(websource, i1)


' First of three read forwards for the sting <td>
```

```vba
    i2 = InStr(1, substr1, findstr2)

    substr2 = Mid(substr1, i2 + 4)


    i3 = InStr(1, substr2, findstr2)

    substr3 = Mid(substr2, i3 + 4)


    i4 = InStr(1, substr3, findstr2)

    substr4 = Mid(substr3, i4 + 4)



' At this point substr4 will be the start of the volume figure

' And we need to read from there until we hit the </td> string

    i5 = InStr(1, substr4, findstr3)

' Now we know the length of string we need to read

    volume = Mid(substr4, 1, i5 - 1)

    MsgBox ("Volume = " & volume)

    Set xmlhttp = Nothing

End Sub
```

Essentially what this code is doing is using xmlhttp to read into a variable the whole of the source of the web page. We then set up three strings to look for that pinpoint exactly the position on the web source data where the three bits of data we're looking for are. After that, it's just some trivial use of a combination of the MID,

INSTR and LEFT text functions to actually get our data. It's quite easy from here to see how this can be extended to grab other data sets from potentially other websites that you might want.

NB You should note that many websites generate the data that you see on their pages "on the fly", as it were, using external programming scripts such as JavaScript for instance. The upshot of this is that when you look at the source for the page you will not see actual data but simply calls to scripts which only fetch the data when you open the web-page in a browser. This means it is often tricky if not impossible to use the method described above. For such websites you might want to consider using a product such as iMacros, the Beautiful Soup python library or the web automation tool Selenium.

The End